THE NEIGHBORHOOD SCHOOL
P.O. BOX 11100
MEMPHIS, TN 38111

— CONTINENTS —

ANTARCTICA

Linda Aspen-Baxter

WEIGL PUBLISHERS INC.

Published by Weigl Publishers Inc.
350 5th Avenue, Suite 3304, PMB 6G
New York, NY USA 10118-0069
Web site: www.weigl.com
Copyright 2006 WEIGL PUBLISHERS INC.

Library of Congress Cataloging-in-Publication Data

Aspen-Baxter, Linda.
  Antarctica / Linda Aspen-Baxter.
     p. cm. -- (Continents)
  Includes index.
  ISBN 1-59036-317-5 (hard cover : alk. paper) -- ISBN 1-59036-324-8 (soft cover :
alk. paper)
  1. Antarctica--Juvenile literature. I. Title. II. Continents (New York, N.Y.)
  G863.A75 2005
  919.8'904--dc22

                                        2005003966

Printed in the United States of America
1 2 3 4 5 6 7 8 9 10 09 08 07 06 05

All of the Internet URLs given in the book were valid at the time of publication. However, due to the dynamic nature of the Internet, some addresses may have changed, or sites may have ceased to exist since publication. While the author and publisher regret any inconvenience this may cause readers, no responsibility for any such changes can be accepted by either the author or the publisher.

Project Coordinator
Heather C. Hudak

Copy Editor
Heather Kissock

Designer
Terry Paulhus

Layout
Gregg Muller
Kathryn Livingstone

Photo Researcher
Kim Winiski

Photograph Credits
Every reasonable effort has been made to trace ownership and to obtain permission
to reprint copyright material. The publishers would be pleased to have any errors
or omissions brought to their attention so that they may be corrected in
subsequent printings.

Cover: Icebergs can be so large that they may take several years to melt.
(Getty Images/Photographer's Choice/Eastcott Momatiuk)

Getty Images: pages 1 (Stone/Kim Westerskov), 4-5 (Robert Harding World
Imagery/David Tipling), 6TR (Stone/Kevin Schafer), 6B (The Image Bank/Eric Meola),
7 (National Geographic/Maria Stenzel), 8 (Taxi/Jonathan & Angela), 9 (Stone/David
Tipling), 10 (Digital Vision), 11 (The Image Bank/Chris Sattlberger), 12 (National
Geographic/Gordon Wiltsie), 13 (Stone/James Martin), 14 (Taxi/Mike Hill), 15 (Robert
Harding World Imagery/Geoff Renner), 16 (Photographer's Choice/Eastcott Momatiuk),
17T (Hulton Archive), 17B (Stock Montage), 18 (Hulton Archive), 19 (Illustrated
London News), 20 (Photographer's Choice/Kim Westerskov), 21 (AFP/Javier Soriano),
22 (National Geographic/Maria Stenzel), 23 (National Geographic/Maria Stenzel), 24
(National Geographic/Gordon Wiltsie), 25 (Picture Post/Hulton Archive), 26
(Stone/Roger Mear), 27 (Lonely Planet Images/Grant Dixon), 28 (Photographer's
Choice/Eastcott Momatiuk), 29TL (National Geographic/Maria Stenzel), 29R (Time
Life Pictures/Mansell/TimeLife Pictures), 29B (National Geographic/Gordon Wiltsie),
30 (Time Life Pictures/Mansell/Time Life Pictures), 32 (Johnny Johnson/Imagebank -
Getty Images).

TABLE OF CONTENTS

Introduction

*A*ntarctica is much more than ice and snow, howling winds, and freezing temperatures. The thick ice sheets of the fifth largest continent could tell stories of brave people who risked their lives to explore this last vast wilderness on Earth.

Millions of years ago, Antarctica was not buried in ice sheets. Scientists have found fossils of trees, dinosaurs, and small mammals that lived on this land long ago. As a result, scientists believe that Antarctica once belonged to a supercontinent called Gondwanaland. Africa, Australia, India, and South America also belonged to this supercontinent. Gondwanaland began breaking apart about 140 million years ago. Its parts drifted to their current locations. Antarctica became the continent that straddles the **South Pole**.

Antarctica is the fifth largest continent. It surrounds the South Pole, and almost all of its land mass is south of the **Antarctic Circle**. The Antarctic Peninsula stretches toward South America, which is 620 miles (1,000 kilometers) away from its tip. Voyages to Antarctica from South America usually leave from Argentina. To reach Antarctica from Tierra del Fuego in Argentina, South America, travelers must cross the Drake Passage. This is the roughest stretch of water in the world. Ships must cross this passage at right angles to the flow of water.

Male and female Adélie penguins take turns incubating, or warming, their eggs until they hatch.

4

Trips to the Ross region and Eastern Antarctica usually leave from the port of Hobart in the Australian state of Tasmania or the ports of Auckland or Christchurch in New Zealand. Australia is 1,550 miles (2,500 kilometers) away from Antarctica. Sometimes ships depart from Cape Town and Port Elizabeth in South Africa for Antarctica. South Africa is 2,500 miles (4,000 km) away.

There are no developed ports or harbors in Antarctica. Ships must anchor offshore. Small boats, barges, and helicopters transfer people and supplies from ships to the shore. There are no developed airports or landing facilities for public airlines. Most antarctic research stations have helicopter pads or aircraft runways made of gravel, sea-ice, or **compacted** snow.

Fast Facts

The **circumpolar current** is so strong in Antarctica that it flows at a rate of about 61,179,402 cubic feet (140,000,000 cubic meters) of water per second. That is the same speed as 5,000 Amazon Rivers.

One of the largest icebergs to separate from the Ross Ice Shelf was 183 miles (295 km) long and 23 miles (37 km) wide. The part of the iceberg that could be seen above the water was about the same size as the state of Connecticut. The iceberg was ten times larger below the water.

Antarctica

The true boundary of Antarctica is not the coastline or the islands that lie off its shores. It is the **Antarctic Convergence**, a strip of water about 25 miles (40 km) wide. Here, the cold waters of the Southern Ocean meet the warmer, saltier waters of the Atlantic, Indian, and Pacific Oceans. Fish and other marine life rarely move across the convergence in antarctic waters.

The South Pole is located near the center of Antarctica on a high, windy plateau of ice and snow. This is where the lines of **longitude** meet in the Southern Hemisphere. The South Pole is 7,825 feet (2,385 meters) above **sea level**. For every 328 feet (100 m) above sea level, the air temperature drops by 1.8° Fahrenheit (1° Celsius). This means the average temperatures of inland locations in Antarctica are 41° F (23° C) below the temperatures at sea level locations on the coast.

Weddell seals can dive 2,000 feet (610 m) deep.

Fast Fact

Antarctic ice sheets hold about 70 percent of the world's fresh water. They hold the greatest volume of fresh water or ice in the world.

Antarctica Continent Map

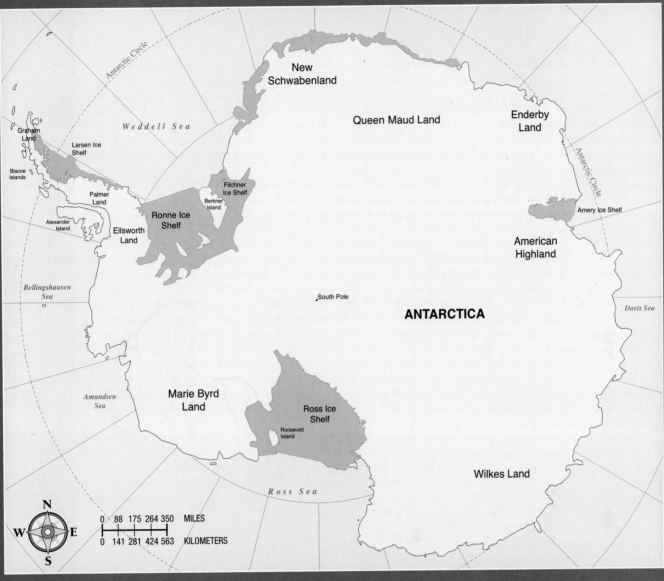

Antarctic Circle

New Schwabenland

Queen Maud Land

Enderby Land

Weddell Sea

Graham Land

Larsen Ice Shelf

Biscoe Islands

Palmer Land

Alexander Island

Ellsworth Land

Filchner Ice Shelf

Berkner Island

Ronne Ice Shelf

Antarctic Circle

Amery Ice Shelf

American Highland

Bellingshausen Sea

South Pole

ANTARCTICA

Davis Sea

Amundsen Sea

Marie Byrd Land

Ross Ice Shelf

Roosevelt Island

Wilkes Land

Ross Sea

N
W · E
S

| 0 | 88 | 175 | 264 | 350 | MILES |
| 0 | 141 | 281 | 424 | 563 | KILOMETERS |

Fast Fact

About 98 percent of Antarctica is covered with ice and snow. If Antarctica's ice sheets melted, the world's oceans would rise by 200 to 230 feet (60 to 70 m).

Location and Resources

Land and Climate

During the warmer summer months, Antarctica covers about 4,700,000 square miles (12,100,000 square kilometers) of land. At the beginning of winter, sea ice along Antarctica's coasts expands by about 40,000 square miles (100,000 sq km) each day. The winter sea ice extends 620 miles (1,000 km) around the continent, adding 7,722,043 square miles (20 million sq km) of ice. In summer, this sea ice breaks into pieces called ice floes, and the continent becomes smaller in size.

Much of Antarctica is a polar desert. Inland Antarctica receives less **precipitation** than the Sahara Desert. Less than 2 inches (5 centimeters) of snow falls each year. Since this snow does not melt or evaporate, it builds up into thick ice sheets.

Some icebergs have an area of 5,000 square miles (13,000 sq km). This is larger than the state of Connecticut.

Antarctica's ice sheets are continuously moving. Huge masses of ice called glaciers form ice shelves along the coasts. In summer, the outer edge of the ice shelves break away to form large, flat icebergs.

The Transantarctic Mountains extend south across the continent from the Antarctic Peninsula. Some peaks in the Transantarctic Mountains are more than 14,000 feet (4,300 m) tall. Dry valleys are found in the Transantarctic Mountains. Glaciers formed these dry, rocky valleys. Strong winds blow the valleys clear of snow and ice.

The Transantarctic Mountains separate Antarctica's ice sheets into sections, creating East Antarctica and West Antarctica. East Antarctica covers more than half of the continent. Mountains, valleys, and glaciers can be seen on East Antarctica's coast. Inland there is a huge ice plateau about 10,000 feet (3,000 m) above sea level, where the South Pole is located. West Antarctica includes deep basin-like areas that lie below sea level. The Antarctic Peninsula stretches from West Antarctica toward South America.

Antarctica is in the Southern Hemisphere, so winter is from June to September. During these months, there is very little sunlight. Winter temperatures range from -94° F to -40° F (-70° C to -40° C) inland. Summer is from November to February, and temperatures range from -31° F to 5° F (-30° C to -21° C) inland. Temperatures can reach 32° F (0° C) on the coast. Antarctica is the coldest and windiest continent.

Fast Facts

Vinson Massif is the highest point in Antarctica. It rises about 16,864 feet (5,140 m).

Mount Erebus on Ross Island is Antarctica's most active volcano. It rises 12,448 feet (3,794 m) above sea level.

The lowest temperature recorded on Earth was -128.6° F (-89.2° C) at the Russian Vostok Station on July 21, 1983.

The lowest known point in Antarctica is the Bentley Subglacial Trench in West Antarctica. It is 8,200 feet (2,499 m) below sea level.

Emperor penguins are the largest penguin species. They live on antarctic pack ice.

Plants and Animals

Trees and bushes do not grow on Antarctica, but there are about 350 species of **lichens**, mosses, and algae. Lichens and mosses cling to bare rock. Black, white, and green lichens grow in cracks in the rocks in dry valleys.

In 1978, biologists discovered algae, fungi, and bacteria growing in Antarctica's dry valleys. These plants grow in air pockets in rocks, where they are protected from the cold, dry winds that sweep the valleys. Algae also grow on snow, lakes, and the ice surrounding Antarctica.

All antarctic **vertebrates** find food in the Southern Ocean or migrate to other continents during the winter. In Antarctica, penguins, such as Adélie and emperor, nest near the shore, spending a great deal of time in the ocean searching for their food. Whales, such as the blue, fin, humpback, and minke, migrate to Antarctica for the summer.

Antarctica's only land animals are tiny **invertebrates**, such as mites, ticks, and nematode worms. During the winter, they live in ice under rocks and stones. Antarctica's largest land animal is an insect called the wingless midge. It is less than 0.5 inches (1.3 cm) long.

More than forty kinds of birds migrate to Antarctica in the summer. Albatrosses, prions, and petrels nest on land. They dive in the ocean for food. Cormorants and terns spend some time on land and steal food from the nests of other birds.

Fast Facts

Only two types of flowering plants grow in Antarctica — Antarctic hair grass and Antarctic pearlwart. Both plants live in the northern part of the Antarctic Peninsula.

Ice fish in the Southern Ocean have no **hemoglobin**. Their blood is clear, and they are a ghostly white color.

Flying insects do not live in Antarctica because the strong winds would blow them away.

Humpback whales live in all of the world's oceans. Most spend their summers in polar regions such as Antarctica. They migrate to warmer tropical waters in the winter.

Natural Resources

It is uncertain what natural resources are buried beneath Antarctica's thick ice sheets. Scientists in Antarctica have found fossils and rock formations similar to those found in South America and South Africa. From this, scientists have concluded that Antarctica may have some of the same natural resources as these other continents. For example, they believe silver, gold, copper, nickel, coal, oil, and natural gas lie beneath the ice. Still, due to the thick layers of ice and snow, scientists do not know for certain which natural resources are available in Antarctica.

Antarctica is home to a large number of whale and seal species. During the nineteenth and early twentieth centuries, hunters killed many whales and Antarctic fur seals. The populations of these animals were greatly reduced. Today, international wildlife laws protect these animals from being overhunted. It is illegal to kill some species, while only a certain number of other species can be hunted.

Fast Facts

Scientists have found samples in exposed rock that give them an idea about what natural resources are available in Antarctica.

Many commercial fishing ships in antarctic waters catch krill, finfish, crab, and squid.

About 98 percent of Antarctica is covered with ice and snow.

Huge ships bring supplies to antarctic research stations. These ships often need the help of icebreakers to move through the frozen waters.

Economy

Tourism

Between November and early December, tourists visit Antarctica to watch the winter pack ice begin to thaw. They can see the mating rituals and dances of the penguins and sea birds on the shores and ice shelves along the coast. While visiting the continent between February and March, tourists can see whales in the ocean waters. At this time of year, there are also adult penguins in their **moulting** stage and larger groups of fur seals on the Antarctic Peninsula.

Deception Island, just north of the Antarctic Peninsula, is a popular stop for tourist ships because the island has an active volcano. Visitors can have a warm bath in Pendulum Cove, where the waters are warmed by heat from volcanic activity. Imagine relaxing in warm waters while surrounded by ice and snow. During the 1920 to 1921 whaling season, there was an eruption. The water in the harbor boiled, and the heat stripped paint off the hulls of ships.

Deception Island is a popular stop for antarctic expeditions. The island is located at the tip of the Antarctic Peninsula.

Paradise Harbor on the Antarctic Peninsula is a great place to watch icebergs break off the glacier. Zodiacs are small inflatable crafts that allow travelers to cruise along the icebergs. Some visitors travel on expeditions outside the Antarctica Peninsula to the Weddell Sea and the Ross Sea. Sometimes, visitors take voyages to the coast of East Antarctica to see emperor penguin colonies. One of the largest penguin colonies in the world awaits visitors on Zavodovski Island on the coast of East Antarctica. About two million chinstrap penguins nest in this location.

The dry valleys of Victoria, Wright, and Taylor feature ice-free spaces called oases. No rain has fallen in these valleys for at least 2 million years. The valleys are large, lonely places covering about 1,170 square miles (3,000 square km).

Most tourists visit Antarctica during the summer months. Ship and tour companies focus on coastal areas that are free of ice. As winter approaches, sea ice begins to form and move. Visitors who come to Antarctica later than March or earlier than November face the very real danger of becoming stuck in sea ice. They may be forced to spend the winter on the continent.

Fast Facts

The cold conditions in Antarctica's dry valleys are similar to Mars's climate. In fact, NASA scientists researched and tested for the *Viking* mission to Mars in these valleys.

The International Association of Antarctic Tour Operators (IAATO) sets environmental protection rules for people visiting Antarctica. For example, only 100 cruise ship or tour passengers may land at any one time and place in Antarctica.

Tourists visiting Antarctica can view wildlife up close.

Industry

Tourism is the fastest growing industry in Antarctica. Each year since the first tourist voyage to Antarctica in the 1960s, more people become interested in visiting the continent. Ships take tourists on 1- to 3-week cruises during which they visit areas on the Antarctic Peninsula or the islands—spending a few hours at each location. Tourists must respect and protect Antarctica's environment.

Commercial mining involves the sale of minerals for profit. Commercial mining is banned in Antarctica. Countries that signed the Antarctic Treaty also signed the Madrid **Protocol**. This protocol, created in 1991, bans mining on the continent for 50 years. Participating countries will review this decision in 2041. There are no known plans to change the decision to ban mining.

Scientific exploration and research are some of the most important activities in Antarctica. Scientists and researchers from different countries live and work at stations on the continent. Research activities include drilling samples of ice known as ice cores. This removes long cylinders of ice. Scientists examine the layers of ice, dust, and air bubbles trapped in the ice to learn about Earth's climate throughout history.

From the hull of a cruise ship, tourists can view the glaciers and icebergs of Antarctica.

Goods and Services

Antarctica does not have any stores, offices, or shops. There are no goods and services offered on the continent. Nations from around the world provide goods and services related to Antarctica. Some companies on other continents sell special clothing and merchandise for people visiting or working on the frigid cold continent. Others, such as tourism groups, host trips to Antarctica. However, these trips originate in other parts of the world. For example, cruise ships that visit ice-free coastal areas travel from Ushuaia, Argentina, Punta Arenas, Chile, Australia, New Zealand, or the Falkland Islands. Tour operators provide detailed information about Antarctica's geography, climate, and history.

Inflatable boats called zodiacs take tourists ashore for antarctic excursions. Zodiacs also allow scientists access to remote areas.

Fast Facts

About twelve cruise lines offer Antarctica voyages. Most Antarctic cruise ships were once icebreakers or research vessels. Most trips last from 1 to 3 weeks.

The Past

Indigenous Peoples

Unlike other continents, Antarctica has no **indigenous peoples**. Antarctica was uninhabited by humans when it was first discovered. Today, there are still no permanent residents of this continent. Scientists who live and work at stations in Antarctica stay for long periods of time, but none of them live there permanently.

Early explorers and hunters were the first people to see Antarctica. The Ancient Greeks believed that a land mass existed at Earth's southern end to balance the weight of the northern lands. As early as the AD 100s, **Ptolemy** gave this land mass the name Terra Australis Incognita, which means unknown southern land. The word Antarctica is a combination of two Greek words that mean "opposite the Bear." The Bear is a **constellation** in the northern hemisphere.

Fast Facts

In November 1820, Nathaniel Brown Palmer, an American sealer, reported that he saw land during a seal hunt.

Some historians believe an American seal hunter named Captain John Davis was the first human to set foot on the continent, when he visited Hughes Bay in 1821. However, Captain Davis was not sure if he had reached the actual continent of Antarctica or an island.

There is more ice and snow in Antarctica than in all the glaciers and snowfields of the rest of the world combined.

Early Explorers

The first explorer to cross the Antarctic Circle was Captain James Cook, in January 1773. He traveled around Antarctica, but he did not see land because of huge icebergs that blocked his view. He knew a southern continent must exist because of the pieces of rock he saw in these icebergs.

In January 1820, Russian naval officer Fabian von Bellingshausen crossed the Antarctic Circle. He sailed around the Antarctic, reaching within 20 miles (32 km) of the Antarctic Peninsula. That same month, British naval officer Captain Edward Bransfield claimed the first sighting of the Antarctic Peninsula.

In 1840, James Clark Ross, a British naval officer and scientist, was the first person to travel beyond the pack ice that surrounded Antarctica. He journeyed within 80 miles (50 km) of the coast of Antarctica. A huge ice barrier blocked him from sailing farther. This barrier is now called the Ross Ice Shelf.

In 1898, Adrien de Gerlache and his crew became the first people to survive an Antarctic winter. Their ship, the *Belgica*, became trapped in pack ice off the Antarctic Peninsula. They drifted with the pack ice through the long winter months.

Fast Facts

Captain Sir James Clark Ross discovered the North Magnetic Pole in 1831.

In 1899, Carsten Borchgrevink and his crew became the first to spend an entire winter on the Antarctic Continent. This British expedition landed at Cape Adare and lived in huts during the winter.

In 1823, James Weddell sailed farther south than any earlier voyages. He reached 74° South latitude and discovered Weddell Sea.

Captain James Cook was the first explorer to cross the Antarctic Circle. He was also the first European to visit New Zealand.

The Age of Heroes

At the beginning of the twentieth century, brave explorers led expeditions to Antarctica hoping to reach the South Pole. Many experienced the thrill of reaching their goals and surviving the challenges of a frozen wilderness. Others experienced the bitter disappointment of being forced to turn back because of harsh weather. Still others lost their lives in their struggle to survive the challenges of exploring Antarctica.

In 1901, British Captain Robert Falcon Scott, with Ernest Shackleton and Edward Wilson, led his first expedition to Antarctica. Their goal was to reach the South Pole. They headed south across the Ross Ice Shelf, but 2 months into their expedition, they suffered from a food shortage, snow blindness, and **scurvy**.

In 1907, Shackleton returned to Antarctica. An Australian named Douglas Mawson led part of Shackleton's expedition in an attempt to reach the South Magnetic Pole, the southernmost point on Earth. Mawson reached this point in January 1909. Shackleton led another expedition team to the South Pole. He journeyed within 97 miles (156 km) of the South Pole before being forced to turn back due to frostbite and a lack of food supplies. By the time they returned to their ship, they had walked 1,700 miles (2,735 km).

Sir Ernest Henry Shackleton first visited Antarctica in 1901, under the command of Captain Robert Scott. Both men wanted to be the first people to reach the South Pole.

Captain Robert Scott left London for the South Pole in June 1910. Soon after, Norwegian explorer Roald Amundsen began his bid to reach the South Pole. The two raced to see who would reach the South Pole first. Amundsen and his team of four left the Bay of Whales on October 19, 1911, and crossed the Ross Ice Shelf. Robert Scott left Cape Evans, Ross Island, on November 1, 1911. When Scott and the four men on his team reached the inland plateau, they set off to reach the South Pole before Amundsen's team.

Amundsen and his team reached the South Pole on December 14, 1911. They left a tent, a Norwegian flag, and a message for Scott before returning to their base. By the time Scott's team reached the South Pole on January 17, 1912, they were suffering from frostbite, hunger, and exhaustion. On their return to base, all five of Scott's team died.

Fast Facts

In 1914, Ernest Shackleton returned to Antarctica. He wanted to make the first crossing of the continent from one coast to the other, via the South Pole. However, his ship was crushed in the sea ice. Twenty-four months and twenty-two days after leaving Great Britain, Shackleton and his crew returned to safety. They did not achieve their goal.

Roald Amundsen marked the South Pole with a Norwegian flag. Today, a monument marks this area. The monument is moved on January 1 of every year because the location of the pole moves slightly.

Culture

Population

In the twentieth century, several countries built scientific bases in Antarctica. People live and work at these bases for a specific period of time. Scientists and support staff can spend from a few months to a couple of years at the bases before they return to their home countries. Then, another group of scientists, researchers, and support staff takes their place to continue the scientific work. Some research stations operate only in summer. Others operate throughout the year.

The population of Antarctica changes during the summer and winter months. In the summer, there can be as many as 20,000 people living on the continent. This total includes more than 5,000 scientists and support workers from 26 countries and the 14,000 or more tourists who visit Antarctica each year. About 4,000 people conduct scientific research on the continent and islands, while about 1,000 people research from on-board ships in the waters of the Southern Ocean. Less than 1,000 people remain in Antarctica during the winter.

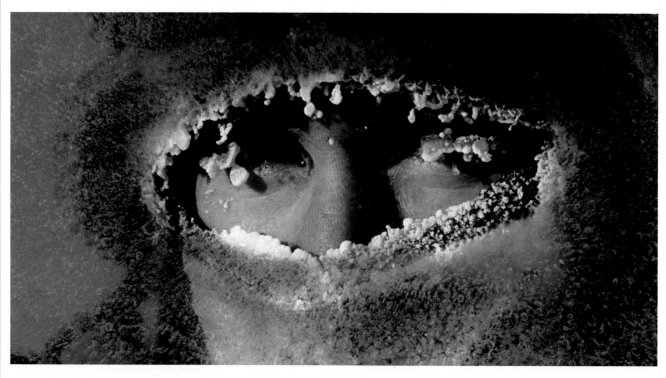

Antarctic field workers must dress for very cold temperatures.

Politics and Government

The International Geophysical Year (IGY) began on July 1, 1957, and ended on December 31, 1958. During this year, thirty-five scientific stations were built on the continent. Twelve different nations also built fifteen stations on the antarctic islands.

Representatives from twelve nations involved in the IGY met in Washington, D.C. in 1959 to create the Antarctic Treaty. The treaty dedicated Antarctica to peaceful scientific investigation and learning. On December 1, 1959, the same twelve countries signed the Antarctic Treaty. The treaty came into effect on June 23, 1961.

When the Antarctic Treaty came into effect, all claims to the continent were **suspended**. In 1991, twenty-four countries approved an addition to the Antarctic Treaty. This addition, called the Madrid Protocol, banned the development of Antarctic oil and other minerals for at least 50 years.

There is no government in Antarctica. The continent is managed by the twenty-seven decision-making countries that follow the terms of the Antarctic Treaty. These countries make decisions by agreement, not by vote.

Fast Facts

The Antarctic Treaty states that soil cannot be brought to Antarctica from other countries. Soil may contain insects, fungi, or bacteria that are not native to the continent.

Seven nations claimed part of Antarctica in the early 1900s. These nations were Argentina, Australia, Chile, France, Great Britain, New Zealand, and Norway.

In June 2003, Spanish State Secretary for International Cooperation Miguel Angel Cortes, Environmental Minister Elvira Rodriguez, and Spanish Prince Felipe de Borbon met with the press during an Antarctic Treaty meeting at the Congress Palace in Madrid.

Cultural Groups

Since there are no indigenous peoples or permanent settlements in Antarctica, the only cultural groups presently residing on the continent are the scientific researchers, stations, and bases from different countries around the world.

The communities at each station are small, and they are **isolated** from one another. These communities work together in emergencies, and they work together to protect the local environment. Scientists also share information. Although they are from different nations, researchers in Antarctica promote peaceful sharing and cooperation. Scientists from different countries even work together on expeditions.

During the summer, groups of scientists and support staff travel far from their stations to field locations. They use radios to keep in contact with their bases. Scientists use helicopters and snow vehicles to carry goods and journey to new locations. Large field teams may include a field leader to plan the daily program, a medical officer, a radio operator to keep in constant contact with the base and aircraft, a **meteorologist** to inform the

The thin atmosphere above Antarctica allows scientists to receive a clear view of space using satellites.

team about the weather, pilots, and aircraft engineers. Teams live in fiberglass huts, which can be easily transported to field locations using a helicopter. They may also live in tents.

At the research bases in Antarctica, people eat frozen, dried, or tinned food for much of the year. Ships and aircraft bring fresh fruit and vegetables to the stations. Some stations grow fresh vegetables using a **hydroponics** system. If there is an outbreak of pests or disease with hydroponics-grown plants, the entire system must be shut down and all plants destroyed.

People on expeditions in the field must eat more to keep warm and to fuel their bodies. In the field, melted snow provides fresh water. Field workers also have to carry the fuel they need to melt the snow and prepare their food. To save fuel, they take food that is quick and easy to prepare. These foods, called sledging rations, are high in fat and **dehydrated**. Sledging rations may include biscuits, butter and cheese, sugar, cocoa, meat and fish, soup, porridge, muesli, vegetables, chocolate, jam, and milk.

Pemmican is a mixture of pounded, dried beef with beef fat. North American Native Peoples first created pemmican. Pemmican provided early Antarctic explorers with nearly half of their daily calories.

Fast Facts

Sledging biscuits from Scott's 1912 expedition to the South Pole and Shackleton's voyage to South Georgia have been auctioned for thousands of dollars over the past few years.

Scurvy was a problem for early explorers. They could not eat the vitamin C-filled fruit and vegetables their bodies needed. Instead, they drank lime or lemon juice.

Antarctic scientists study **global warming**. They observe its affects on nematode worms living in the antarctic soil.

Arts and Entertainment

The people at research stations need to take breaks from working. In their **leisure** time, they read books, watch movies, and listen to music. They also surf the Internet and e-mail their family and friends. Some create artwork, while others enjoy woodworking projects.

Expeditions that are spending the winter in Antarctica sometimes hold darts and chess competitions over the radio. People at bases from other countries visit with each other over the radio. They may also visit each other's stations. In the spring and summer months, people take trips to places away from the stations. They sometimes stay the night in huts or tents. Many people enjoy watching and photographing penguins and seals.

Climbing is a popular activity for antarctic scientists and adventurers. With peaks approaching 16,000 feet (5,000 m) high, Antarctica is ideal for climbing.

The most important event and holiday in Antarctica is Midwinter Day, which takes place on June 21 or 22. On this day, people celebrate because the winter is half over. Everyone who remains in Antarctica for the winter celebrates this day. People enjoy feasting, games, songs, and even theater or musical productions at the bases. Midwinter Day has been celebrated since the early 1900s, when Shackleton, Scott, and Mawson explored the continent.

Many documentaries have been made about Antarctica. A short film titled *The White Continent* was released in 1951. It followed the members of a Norwegian, British, and Swedish expedition.

Fast Facts

June 21 is the darkest day in Antarctica. After this day, a long period of darkness is broken by glimpses of sunlight.

Some people film documentaries in Antarctica. The 1991 film *Antarctica*, directed by John Weiley, describes the continent and its explorers.

Sports

*I*t is difficult to play outdoor sports in Antarctica because of the extremely cold weather. Instead, research stations provide indoor gymnasiums, and volleyball and basketball courts for their staff. Many people also enjoy cross-country skiing, jogging, and walking. Another favorite activity is playing snooker or darts.

With the proper qualifications, tourists and scientists can SCUBA dive in the waters along the coasts of Antarctica. However, most SCUBA operators only allow divers to go between 30 and 60 feet (9 and 18 m) below the surface. To dive deeper poses life-threatening danger due to **compression**. Some tourists have the opportunity to camp on the shore. They can also take hikes. Some even climb the rocky land, hills, and terrain. In 1995, more than 100 runners participated in the first Antarctic Marathon. The marathon took place on King George Island. It featured

Adventurers often hike for days across Antarctica, hoping to be one of the few to reach the South Pole on foot.

a 26-mile (42-km) double-loop course. The runners began at the Uruguayan base. They had to pass through the Russian, Chilean, and Chinese stations on this island. Some of the runners became **delirious** with **hypothermia**. Other runners became lost in the fog on the top of a glacier. One runner even fell in a **crevasse** up to his chest.

In December 2003, a British boating company began organizing a yacht race around Antarctica. Sailing in 85-foot (26-m) yachts, participants raced above and below the Antarctic Convergence—a distance of 14,600 nautical miles (27,000 km). Beginning in Auckland, New Zealand, countries compete against each other in a race to the finish. The first race, called the Antarctic Cup, took place in February 2005. The Antarctic Cup will take place every 2 years.

Fast Facts

Each nation competing in the Antarctic Cup races in an identical yacht. This eliminates design advantages—giving each team an equal start in the race.

During the last half of the twentieth century, Antarctica's emperor penguin population declined by 50 percent.

Many areas in Antarctica are named after early explorers and adventurers. Shackleton Gap (pictured here), the Ross Ice Shelf, and the Weddell Sea are just a few.

Brain Teasers

 1 What is the name of the stretch of water that must be crossed to travel to Antarctica from South America?

 2 What is found near the center of Antarctica?

 3 What is on Deception Island that warms the water in Pendulum Cove?

4 What are the only land animals in Antarctica?

5 When is winter in Antarctica?

 6 What happens to the area of Antarctica in winter?

 7 What agreement helps twenty-seven countries manage Antarctica?

8 Which kinds of plants grow in Antarctica?

9 Who lives in Antarctica permanently?

10 Who led the expedition that reached the South Pole first?

For More Information

Books

Check the school or public library for more information about Antarctica. The following books have useful information about the continent:

Armstrong, Jennifer. *Shipwreck at the Bottom of the World: The Extraordinary and True Story of Shackleton and the Endurance.* New York: Crown Books for Young Readers, 1998.

Myers, Walter Dean. *Antarctica: Journeys to the South Pole.* New York: Scholastic Press, 2004.

Wheeler, Sara. *Greetings from Antarctica.* New York: Peter Bedrick, 2001.

Web sites

You can also go online and have a look at the following Web sites:

Cool Antarctica
www.coolantarctica.com

Australia Antarctic Division
www.antdiv.gov.au.

Antarctica Online
www.antarcticaonline.com/antarctica/home/home.htm

Glacier
www.glacier.rice.edu

British Antarctic Survey
www.antarctica.ac.uk

Glossary

Antarctic Circle a line of latitude north of the South Pole

Antarctic Convergence a strip of water about 25 miles (40 km) wide that wraps around Antarctica; a place where the cold waters of the Southern Ocean meet the warmer, saltier waters of the Atlantic, Indian, and Pacific Oceans

circumpolar current a strong current that flows east to west around Antarctica

compacted firmly packed

compression the act of pressing together or flattening

constellation a formation of stars that looks like a figure or shape

crevasse a deep, narrow opening caused by a split or a crack in a glacier

dehydrated to have the water content removed

delirious to be in a state of confusion

global warming an increase in the world's temperatures

hemoglobin an iron-containing substance in red blood cells

hydroponics where plants grow in slowly circulating water that is filled with nutrients

hypothermia to suffer from a very low body temperature

indigenous peoples original inhabitants of an area

invertebrates animals without a backbone

isolated to be separated from others

leisure time off from work and other duties; free time

lichens fungi that grow with algae

longitude imaginary lines measuring east to west around Earth

meteorologist a person who studies the atmosphere and forecasts weather

moulting shedding of skin

precipitation any form of water, such as rain or snow, that falls to Earth's surface

protocol the proper code of conduct or way to behave

Ptolemy an ancient astronomer who believed stars rotated around Earth

scurvy a disease caused by lack of vitamin C, which causes bleeding from the gums, loosening of the teeth, bleeding into muscles and joints, and pain

sea level the surface level of the sea midway between high and low tide

South Pole the point at which all the lines of longitude meet in the southern hemisphere; the south geographic pole

suspended stopped for a period of time

vertebrates animals with backbones

Index